RILEY LOVE-LYRICS

BOOKS BY JAMES WHITCOMB RILEY

Neghborly Poems.

Sketches in Prose with Interluding Verses.

Afterwhiles.

Pipes o' Pan at Zekesbury (Prose and Verse).

Rhymes of Childhood.

The Flying Islands of the Night.

Green Fields and Running Brooks.

Armazindy.

A Child-World.

Home-Folks.

His Pa's Romance (Portrait by Clay).

GREENFIELD EDITION

Sold only in sets. Twelve volumes uniformly bound in sage-green cloth, gilt top, $15.00

The same in limp leather, net 18.00
The same in half-calf..... 27.00

The Lockerbie Book of Riley Verse (Containing all Poems not in Dialect).

Old-Fashioned Roses (English Edition).

The Golden Year (English Edition).

Poems Here at Home (Pictures by Relyea).

Rubáiyát of Doc Sifers (Pictures by Kemble).

The Book of Joyous Children.

Knee Deep in June.

A Summer's Day.

The Prayer Perfect.

The Old Swimmin' Hole.

Down Around the River.

When the Frost is on the Punkin.

Riley Child-Rhymes (Pictures by Vawter).

Riley Love-Lyrics (Pictures by Dyer).

Riley Farm-Rhymes (Pictures by Vawter).

Riley Songs o' Cheer (Pictures by Vawter).

Riley Songs of Summer (Pictures by Vawter).

Riley Songs of Home (Pictures by Vawter).

An Old Sweetheart of Mine (Pictures by Christy).

Out to Old Aunt Mary's (Pictures by Christy).

Home Again with Me (Pictures by Christy).

The Girl I Loved (Pictures by Christy).

When She Was About Sixteen (Pictures by Christy).

Riley Roses (Pictures by Christy).

A Defective Santa Claus (Forty Pictures by Relyea and Vawter).

The Boys of the Old Glee Club (Pictures by Vawter).

Old School Day Romances (Pictures by Crawford).

A Hoosier Romance (Pictures by Adams).

All the Year Round (Wood-cuts by Baumann).

While the Heart Beats Young (Pictures by Betts).

Riley Child Verse (Pictures by Betts).

The Runaway Boy (Pictures by Betts).

The Raggedy Man (Pictures by Betts).

Little Orphant Annie (Pictures by Betts).

Ef You Don't Watch Out (Pictures by Betts).

The Boy Lives On Our Farm (Pictures by Betts).

RILEY

LOVE-LYRICS

JAMES WHITCOMB RILEY

WITH

LIFE PICTURES

BY

WILLIAM B. DYER

RILEY

LOVE-LYRICS

JAMES WHITCOMB RILEY

WITH

LIFE PICTURES

BY

WILLIAM B. DYER

INDIANAPOLIS
THE BOBBS-MERRILL COMPANY
PUBLISHERS

CHARLES FRANCIS PRESS, NEW YORK

INSCRIBED

To the Elect of Love,—or side-by-side
In raptest ecstasy, or sundered wide
By seas that bear no message to or fro
Between the loved and lost of long ago.

SO were I but a minstrel, deft
　　At weaving, with the trembling strings
Of my glad harp, the warp and weft
　　Of rondels such as rapture sings,—
　　　　I'd loop my lyre across my breast,
　　　　Nor stay me till my knee found rest
　　　　In midnight banks of bud and flower
　　　　Beneath my lady's lattice-bower.

And there, drenched with the teary dews,
　　I'd woo her with such wondrous art
As well might stanch the songs that ooze
　　Out of the mockbird's breaking heart;
　　　　So light, so tender, and so sweet
　　　　Should be the words I would repeat,
　　　　Her casement, on my gradual sight,
　　　　Would blossom as a lily might.

CONTENTS

CONTENTS—*Continued*

ILLUSTRATIONS

ILLUSTRATIONS—*Continued*

ILLUSTRATIONS—*Continued*

ILLUSTRATIONS—*Continued*

RILEY LOVE-LYRICS

AN OLD SWEETHEART OF MINE

A S ONE who cons at evening o'er an album all
alone,
And muses on the faces of the friends that he has known,
So I turn the leaves of fancy till, in shadowy design,
I find the smiling features of an old sweetheart of mine.

The lamplight seems to glimmer with a flicker of surprise,
As I turn it low to rest me of the dazzle in my eyes,
And light my pipe in silence, save a sigh that seems to
    yoke
Its fate with my tobacco and to vanish with the smoke.

'Tis a fragrant retrospection—for the loving thoughts
    that start
Into being are like perfume from the blossom of the
    heart;
And to dream the old dreams over is a luxury divine—
When my truant fancy wanders with that old sweetheart
    of mine.

24

Though I hear, beneath my study, like a fluttering of
      wings,
The voices of my children, and the mother as she sings,
I feel no twinge of conscience to deny me any theme
When Care has cast her anchor in the harbor of a dream.

In fact, to speak in earnest, I believe it adds a charm
To spice the good a trifle with a little dust of harm—
For I find an extra flavor in Memory's mellow wine
That makes me drink the deeper to that old sweetheart
      of mine.

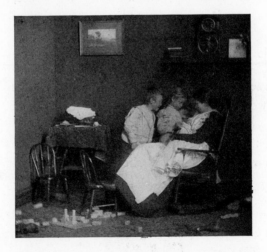

A face of lily-beauty, with a form of airy grace,
Floats out of my tobacco as the genii from the vase;
And I thrill beneath the glances of a pair of azure eyes
As glowing as the summer and as tender as the skies.

I can see the pink sunbonnet and the little checkered dress
She wore when first I kissed her and she answered the
    caress
With the written declaration that, "as surely as the vine
Grew round the stump," she loved me—that old sweet-
    heart of mine.

And again I feel the pressure of her slender little hand,
As we used to talk together of the future we had
    planned—

26

When I should be a poet, and with nothing else to do
But write the tender verses that she set the music to:

When we should live together in a cozy little cot
Hid in a nest of roses, with a fairy garden-spot,
Where the vines were ever fruited, and the weather ever
     fine,
And the birds were ever singing for that old sweetheart
     of mine:

When I should be her lover forever and a day,
And she my faithful sweetheart till the golden hair was
     gray;
And we should be so happy that when either's lips were
     dumb
They would not smile in Heaven till the other's kiss had
     come.

    *   *   *   *   *   *   *   *

But, as! my dream is broken by a step upon the stair,
And the door is softly opened, and—my wife is standing
there;
Yet with eagerness and rapture all my visions I resign
To greet the living presence of that old sweetheart of
mine.

A' OLD PLAYED-OUT SONG

IT'S the curiousest thing in creation,
    Whenever I hear that old song
"Do They Miss Me at Home," I'm so bothered,
    My life seems as short as it's long!—
Fer ev'rything 'pears like adzackly
    It 'peared in the years past and gone,—
When I started out sparkin', at twenty,
    And had my first neckercher on!

Though I'm wrinkelder, older and grayer
    Right now than my parents was then,
You strike up that song "Do They Miss Me,"
    And I'm jest a youngster again!—
I'm a-standin' back thare in the furries
    A-wishin' fer evening to come,
And a-whisperin' over and over
    Them words "Do They Miss Me at Home?"

You see, *Marthy Ellen she* sung it
    The first time I heerd it; and so,

As she was my very first sweetheart,
    It reminds me of her, don't you know;—
How her face used to look, in the twilight,
    As I tuck her to Spellin'; and she
Kep' a-hummin' that song tel I ast her,
    Pine-blank, ef she ever missed *me!*

I can shet my eyes now, as you sing it,
    And hear her low answerin' words;
And then the glad chirp of the crickets,
    As clear as the twitter of birds;
And the dust in the road is like velvet,
    And the ragweed and fennel and grass
Is as sweet as the scent of the lilies
    Of Eden of old, as we pass.

"Do They Miss Me at Home?" Sing it lower—
    And softer—and sweet as the breeze
That powdered our path with the snowy
    White bloom of the old locus'-trees!
Let the whipperwills he'p you to sing it,
    And the echoes 'way over the hill,
Tel the moon boolges out, in a chorus
    Of stars, and our voices is still.

32

But oh! "They's a chord in the music
    That's missed when *her* voice is away!"
Though I listen from midnight tel morning,
    And dawn tel the dusk of the day!
And I grope through the dark, lookin' up'ards
    And on through the heavenly dome,
With my longin' soul singin' and sobbin'
    The words "Do They Miss Me at Home?"

A VERY YOUTHFUL AFFAIR

I'M bin a-visitun 'bout a week
  To my little Cousin's at Nameless Creek,
An' I'm got the hives an' a new straw hat,
An' I'm come back home where my beau lives at.

36

AN OUT-WORN SAPPHO

HOW tired I am! I sink down all alone
   Here by the wayside of the Present. Lo,
Even as a child I hide my face and moan—
   A little girl that may no farther go;
   The path above me only seems to grow
     More rugged, climbing still, and ever briered
   With keener thorns of pain than these below;
   And O the bleeding feet that falter so
     And are so very tired!

Why, I have journeyed from the far-off Lands
   Of Babyhood—where baby-lilies blew
Their trumpets in mine ears, and filled my hands
   With treasures of perfume and honey-dew,
   And where the orchard shadows ever drew
     Their cool arms round me when my cheeks were fired
   With too much joy, and lulled mine eyelids to,
   And only let the starshine trickle through
     In sprays, when I was tired!

Yet I remember, when the butterfly
　Went flickering about me like a flame
That quenched itself in roses suddenly,
　　How oft I wished that *I* might blaze the same,
　　And in some rose-wreath nestle with my name,
　　　While all the world looked on it and admired.—
　Poor moth!—Along my wavering flight toward fame
　The winds drive backward, and my wings are lame
　　　And broken, bruised and tired!

I hardly know the path from those old times;
　I know at first it was a smoother one
Than this that hurries past me now, and climbs
　　So high, its far cliffs even hide the sun
　　And shroud in gloom my journey scarce begun.
　　　I could not do quite all the world required—
　I could not do quite all I should have done,
　And in my eagerness I have outrun
　　　My strength—and I am tired. . . .

Just tired! But when of old I had the stay
　Of mother-hands, O very sweet indeed
It was to dream that all the weary way
　　I should but follow where I now must lead—

38

For long ago they left me in my need,
　And, groping on alone, I tripped and mired
Among rank grasses where the serpents breed
In knotted coils about the feet of speed.—
　　There first it was I tired.

And yet I staggered on, and bore my load
　Right gallantly: The sun, in summer-time,
In lazy belts came slipping down the road
　To woo me on, with many a glimmering rhyme
　Rained from the golden rim of some fair clime,
　　That, hovering beyond the clouds, inspired
My failing heart with fancies so sublime
I half forgot my path of dust and grime,
　　Though I was growing tired.

And there were many voices cheering me:
　I listened to sweet praises where the wind
Went laughing o'er my shoulders gleefully
　And scattering my love-songs far behind;—
　Until, at last, I thought the world so kind—
　　So rich in all my yearning soul desired—
So generous—so loyally inclined,
I grew to love and trust it. . . . I was blind—
　　Yea, blind as I was tired!

And yet óne hand held me in creature-touch:
　And O, how fair it was, how true and strong,
How it did hold my heart up like a crutch,
　Till, in my dreams, I joyed to walk along
　The toilsome way, contented with a song—
　　'Twas all of earthly things I had acquired,
　And 'twas enough, I feigned, or right or wrong,
　Since, binding me to man—a mortal thong—
　　It stayed me, growing tired. . . .

Yea, I had e'en resigned me to the strait
　Of earthly rulership—had bowed my head
Acceptant of the master-mind—the great
　One lover—lord of all,—the perfected
　Kiss-comrade of my soul;—had stammering said
　　My prayers to him;—all—all that he desired
　I rendered sacredly as we were wed.—
　Nay—nay!—'twas but a myth I worshippéd.—
　　And—God of love!—how tired!

For, O my friends, to lose the latest grasp—
　To feel the last hope slipping from its hold—
To feel the one fond hand within your clasp
　Fall slack, and loosen with a touch so cold

Its pressure may not warm you as of old
   Before the light of love had thus expired—
To know your tears are worthless, though they rolled
Their torrents out in molten drops of gold.—
     God's pity! I am tired!

And I must rest.—Yet do not say "She *died*,"·
   In speaking of me, sleeping here alone.
I kiss the grassy grave I sink beside,
   And close mine eyes in slumber all mine own:
   Hereafter I shall neither sob nor moan
     Nor murmur one complaint;—all I desired,
   And failed in life to find, will now be known—
So let me dream. Good night! And on the stone
     Say simply: She was tired.

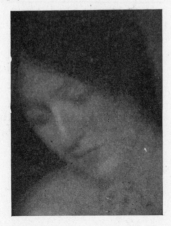

THE PASSING OF A HEART

O TOUCH me with your hands—
　　　　　　　　For pity's sake!
My brow throbs ever on with such an ache
As only your cool touch may take away;
And so, I pray
　　　　　　　You, touch me with your hands!

Touch—touch me with your hands.—
　　　　　　　　Smooth back the hair
You once caressed, and kissed, and called so fair
That I did dream its gold would wear alway,
And lo, to-day—
　　　　　　　O touch me with your hands!

44

Just touch me with your hands,

                      And let them press
My weary eyelids with the old caress,
And lull me till I sleep. Then go your way,
That Death may say:
              He touched her with his hands.

"DREAM"

BECAUSE her eyes were far too deep
        And holy for a laugh to leap
Across the brink where sorrow tried
To drown within the amber tide;
Because the looks, whose ripples kissed
The trembling lids through tender mist,
Were dazzled with a radiant gleam—
Because of this I called her "Dream."

Because the roses growing wild
About her features when she smiled
Were ever dewed with tears that fell
With tenderness ineffable;
Because her lips might spill a kiss
That, dripping in a world like this,
Would tincture death's myrrh-bitter stream
To sweetness—so I called her "Dream."

Because I could not understand
The magic touches of a hand

That seemed, beneath her strange control,
To smooth the plumage of the soul
And calm it, till, with folded wings,
It half forgot its flutterings,
And, nestled in her palm, did seem
To trill a song that called her "Dream."

Because I saw her, in a sleep
As dark and desolate and deep
And fleeting as the taunting night
That flings a vision of delight
To some lorn martyr as he lies
In slumber ere the day he dies—
Because she vanished like a gleam
Of glory, do I call her "Dream."

HE CALLED HER IN

I

HE called her in from me and shut the door.
  And she so loved the sunshine and the sky!—
She loved them even better yet than I
That ne'er knew dearth of them—my mother dead,
Nature had nursed me in her lap instead:
And I had grown a dark and eerie child
That rarely smiled,
Save when, shut all alone in grasses high,
Looking straight up in God's great lonesome sky
And coaxing Mother to smile back on me.
'Twas lying thus, this fair girl suddenly
Came to me, nestled in the fields beside
A pleasant-seeming home, with doorway wide—
The sunshine beating in upon the floor

Like golden rain.—
O sweet, sweet face above me, turn again
And leave me! I had cried, but that an ache
Within my throat so gripped it I could make
No sound but a thick sobbing. Cowering so,
I felt her light hand laid
Upon my hair—a touch that ne'er before
Had tamed me thus, all soothed and unafraid—
It seemed the touch the children used to know
When Christ was here, so dear it was—so dear,—-
At once I loved her as the leaves love dew
In midmost summer when the days are new.
Barely an hour I knew her, yet a curl
Of silken sunshine did she clip for me
Out of the bright May-morning of her hair,
And bound and gave it to me laughingly,
And caught my hands and called me *"Little girl,"*
Tiptoeing, as she spoke, to kiss me there!
And I stood dazed and dumb for very stress
Of my great happiness.
She plucked me by the gown, nor saw how mean
The raiment—drew me with her everywhere:
Smothered her face in tufts of grasses green:
Put up her dainty hands and peeped between
Her fingers at the blossoms—crooned and talked
To them in strange, glad whispers, as we walked,—-
Said *this* one was her angel mother—*this,*
Her baby-sister—come back, for a kiss,

53

Clean from the Good-World!—smiled and kissed them,
    then
Closed her soft eyes and kissed them o'er again.
And so did she beguile me—so we played,—
She was the dazzling Shine—I, the dark Shade—
And we did mingle like to these, and thus,
Together, made
The perfect summer, pure and glorious.
So blent we, till a harsh voice broke upon
Our happiness.—She, startled as a fawn,
Cried, "Oh, 'tis Father!"—all the blossoms gone
From out her cheeks as those from out her grasp.—
Harsher the voice came:—She could only gasp
Affrightedly, "Good-bye!—good-bye! good-bye!"
And lo, I stood alone, with that harsh cry
Ringing a new and unknown sense of shame
Through soul and frame,
And, with wet eyes, repeating o'er and o'er,—
"He called her in from me and shut the door!"

II

He called her in from me and shut the door!
And I went wandering alone again—
So lonely—O so very lonely then,

I thought no little sallow star, alone
In all a world of twilight, e'er had known
Such utter loneliness. But that I wore
Above my heart that gleaming tress of hair
To lighten up the night of my despair,
I think I might have groped into my grave
Nor cared to wave
The ferns above it with a breath of prayer.
And how I hungered for the sweet, sweet face
That bent above me in my hiding-place
That day amid the grasses there beside
Her pleasant home!—"Her *pleasant* home!" I sighed,
Remembering;—then shut my teeth and feigned
The harsh voice calling *me,*—then clinched my nails
So deeply in my palms, the sharp wounds pained,
And tossed my face toward heaven, as one who pales
In splendid martyrdom, with soul serene,
As near to God as high the guillotine.
And I had *envied* her? Not that—O no!
But I had longed for some sweet haven so!—
Wherein the tempest-beaten heart might ride
Sometimes at peaceful anchor, and abide
Where those that loved me touched me with their hands,
And looked upon me with glad eyes, and slipped

55

Smooth fingers o'er my brow, and lulled the strands
Of my wild tresses, as they backward tipped
My yearning face and kissed it satisfied.
Then bitterly I murmured as before,—
"He called her in from me and shut the door!"

III

He called her in from me and shut the door!
After long struggling with my pride and pain—
A weary while it seemed, in which the more
I held myself from her, the greater fain
Was I to look upon her face again;—
At last—at last—half conscious where my feet
Were faring, I stood waist-deep in the sweet
Green grasses there where she
First came to me.—
The very blossoms she had plucked that day,
And, at her father's voice, had cast away,
Around me lay,
Still bright and blooming in these eyes of mine;
And as I gathered each one eagerly,
I pressed it to my lips and drank the wine
Her kisses left there for the honey-bee.
Then, after I had laid them with the tress

Of her bright hair with lingering tenderness,
I, turning, crept on to the hedge that bound
Her pleasant-seeming home—but all around
Was never sign of her!—The windows all
Were blinded; and I heard no rippling fall
Of her glad laugh, nor any harsh voice call;—
But clutching to the tangled grasses, caught
A sound as though a strong man bowed his head
And sobbed alone—unloved—uncomforted!—
And then straightway before
My tearless eyes, all vividly, was wrought
A vision that is with me evermore:—
A little girl that lies asleep, nor hears
Nor heeds not any voice nor fall of tears.—
And I sit singing o'er and o'er and o'er,—
"God called her in from him and shut the door!"

HER BEAUTIFUL EYES

O HER beautiful eyes! they are blue as the dew
On the violet's bloom when the morning is new,
And the light of their love is the gleam of the sun
O'er the meadows of Spring where the quick shadows
run
As the morn shifts the mists and the clouds from the
skies—
So I stand in the dawn of her beautiful eyes.

And her beautiful eyes are as mid-day to me,
When the lily-bell bends with the weight of the bee,
And the throat of the thrush is a-pulse in the heat,
And the senses are drugged with the subtle and sweet
And delirious breaths of the air's lullabies—
So I swoon in the noon of her beautiful eyes.

O her beautiful eyes! they have smitten mine own
As a glory glanced down from the glare of the Thron
And I reel, and I falter and fall, as afar
Fell the shepherds that looked on the mystical Star,
And yet dazed in the tidings that bade them arise—
So I groped through the night of her beautiful eyes.

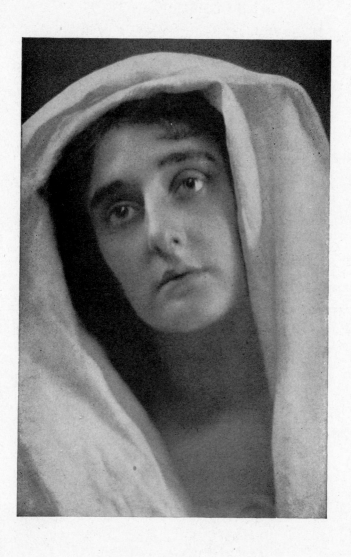

HER FACE AND BROW

A H, help me! but her face and brow
    Are lovelier than lilies are
Beneath the light of moon and star
That smile as they are smiling now—
White lilies in a pallid swoon
Of sweetest white beneath the moon—
White lilies, in a flood of bright
Pure lucidness of liquid light
Cascading down some plenilune,
When all the azure overhead
Blooms like a dazzling daisy-bed.—
So luminous her face and brow,
The luster of their glory, shed
In memory, even, blinds me now.

LET US FORGET

LET us forget. What matters it that we
　　Once reigned o'er happy realms of long-ago,
　And talked of love, and let our voices low,
And ruled for some brief sessions royally?
What if we sung, or laughed, or wept maybe?
　It has availed not anything, and so
　Let it go by that we may better know
How poor a thing is lost to you and me.
　But yesterday I kissed your lips, and yet
Did thrill you not enough to shake the dew
　From your drenched lids—and missed, with no regret,
Your kiss shot back, with sharp breaths failing you:
　And so, to-day, while our worn eyes are wet
　With all this waste of tears, let us forget!

WHEN SHE COMES HOME

WHEN she comes home again! A thousand **ways**
    I fashion, to myself, the tenderness
Of my glad welcome: I shall tremble—yes;
And touch her, as when first in the old days
I touched her girlish hand, nor dared upraise
    Mine eyes, such was my faint heart's sweet **distress**
    Then silence: And the perfume of her dress:
The room will sway a little, and a haze
    Cloy eyesight—soulsight, even—for a space:
And tears—yes; and the ache here in the throat,
    To know that I so ill deserve the place
Her arms make for me; and the sobbing note
    I stay with kisses, ere the tearful face
    Again is hidden in the old embrace.

LEONAINIE

LEONAINIE—Angels named her;
And they took the light
Of the laughing stars and framed her
In a smile of white;

And they made her hair of gloomy
Midnight, and her eyes of bloomy
Moonshine, and they brought her to me
In the solemn night.—

In a solemn night of summer,
When my heart of gloom
Blossomed up to greet the comer
Like a rose in bloom;
All forebodings that distressed me
I forgot as Joy caressed me—
(*Lying* Joy! that caught and pressed me
In the arms of doom!)

Only spake the little lisper
In the Angel-tongue;
Yet I, listening, heard her whisper—
"Songs are only sung
Here below that they may grieve you—
Tales but told you to deceive you,—
So must Leonainie leave you
While her love is young."

69

Then God smiled and it was morning.
  Matchless and supreme
Heaven's glory seemed adorning
  Earth with its esteem:
      Every heart but mine seemed gifted
      With the voice of prayer, and lifted
      Where my Leonainie drifted
  From me like a dream.

HER WAITING FACE

In some strange place
Of long-lost lands he finds her waiting face—
Comes marveling upon it, unaware,
Set moonwise in the midnight of her hair.

71

THE OLD YEAR AND THE NEW

I

AS one in sorrow looks upon
    The dead face of a loyal friend,
By the dim light of New Year's dawn
    I saw the Old Year end.

Upon the pallid features lay
    The dear old smile—so warm and bright
Ere thus its cheer had died away
    In ashes of delight.

The hands that I had learned to love
    With strength of passion half divine,
Were folded now, all heedless of
    The emptiness of mine.

The eyes that once had shed their bright
   Sweet looks like sunshine, now were dull,
And ever lidded from the light
   That made them beautiful.

II

The chimes of bells were in the air,
   And sounds of mirth in hall and street,
With pealing laughter everywhere
   And throb of dancing feet:

The mirth and the convivial din
   Of revelers in wanton glee,
With tunes of harp and violin
   In tangled harmony.

But with a sense of nameless dread,
   I turned me, from the merry face
Of this newcomer, to my dead;
   And, kneeling there a space,

I sobbed aloud, all tearfully:—
   By this dear face so fixed and cold,
O Lord, let not this New Year be
   As happy as the old!

THEIR SWEET SORROW

THEY meet to say farewell: Their way
   Of saying this is hard to say.—
He holds her hand an instant, wholly
Distressed—and she unclasps it slowly.

He bends *his* gaze evasively
Over the printed page that she
   Recurs to, with a new-moon shoulder
   Glimpsed from the lace-mists that enfold her.

The clock, beneath its crystal cup,
Discreetly clicks—*"Quick! Act! Speak up!"*
   A tension circles both her slender
   Wrists—and her raised eyes flash in splendor,

Even as he feels his dazzled own.—
Then, blindingly, round either thrown,
   They feel a stress of arms that ever
   Strain tremblingly—and *"Never! Never!"*

Is whispered brokenly, with half
A sob, like a belated laugh,—
   While cloyingly their blurred kiss closes,
   Sweet as the dew's lip to the rose's.

JUDITH

O HER eyes are amber-fine—
   Dark and deep as wells of wine.
While her smile is like the noon
Splendor of a day of June.
If she sorrow—lo! her face
It is like a flowery space

79

In bright meadows, overlaid
With light clouds and lulled with shade.
If she laugh—it is the trill
Of the wayward whippoorwill
Over upland pastures, heard
Echoed by the mocking-bird
In dim thickets dense with bloom
And blurred cloyings of perfume.
If she sigh—a zephyr swells
Over odorous asphodels
And wan lilies in lush plots
Of moon-drown'd forget-me-nots.
Then, the soft touch of her hand—
Takes all breath to understand
What to liken it thereto!—
Never roseleaf rinsed with dew
Might slip soother-suave than slips
Her slow palm, the while her lips
Swoon through mine, with kiss on kiss
Sweet as heated honey is.

HE AND I

JUST drifting on together—
    He and I—
As through the balmy weather
    Of July
  Drift two thistle-tufts imbedded
  Each in each—by zephyrs wedded—
  Touring upward, giddy-headed,
    For the sky.

And, veering up and onward,
    Do we seem
Forever drifting dawnward
    In a dream,
  Where we meet song-birds that know us
  And the winds their kisses blow us,
  While the years flow far below us
    Like a stream.

And we are happy—very—
    He and I—

Aye, even glad and merry
    Though on high
The heavens are sometimes shrouded
By the midnight storm, and clouded
Till the pallid moon is crowded
    From the sky.

My spirit ne'er expresses
    Any choice
But to clothe him with caresses
    And rejoice;
And as he laughs, it is in
Such a tone the moonbeams glisten
And the stars come out to listen
    To his voice.

And so, whate'er the weather,
    He and I,—
With our lives linked thus together,
    Float and fly
As two thistle-tufts imbedded
Each in each—by zephyrs wedded—
Touring upward, giddy-headed,
    For the sky.

THE LOST PATH

ALONE they walked—their fingers knit together,
  And swaying listlessly as might a swing
Wherein Dan Cupid dangled in the weather
Of some sun-flooded afternoon of Spring.

Within the clover-fields the tickled cricket
  Laughed lightly as they loitered down the lane,
And from the covert of the hazel-thicket
  The squirrel peeped and laughed at them again.

The bumble-bee that tipped the lily-vases
  Along the road-side in the shadows dim,
Went following the blossoms of their faces
  As though their sweets must needs be shared with him

Between the pasture bars the wondering cattle
  Stared wistfully, and from their mellow bells
Shook out a welcoming whose dreamy rattle
  Fell swooningly away in faint farewells.

And though at last the gloom of night fell o'er them
  And folded all the landscape from their eyes,
They only know the dusky path before them
  Was leading safely on to Paradise.

MY BRIDE THAT IS TO BE

O SOUL of mine, look out and see
 My bride, my bride that is to be!
Reach out with mad, impatient hands,
And draw aside futurity
As one might draw a veil aside—
 And so unveil her where she stands
Madonna-like and glorified—
 The queen of undiscovered lands
Of love, to where she beckons me—
My bride—my bride that is to be.

The shadow of a willow-tree
 That wavers on a garden-wall
 In summertime may never fall
In attitude as gracefully
As my fair bride that is to be;—
 Nor ever Autumn's leaves of brown
As lightly flutter to the lawn
As fall her fairy-feet upon
 The path of love she loiters down.—
O'er drops of dew she walks, and yet
Not one may stain her sandal wet—

Aye, she might *dance* upon the way
Nor crush a single drop to spray,
So airy-like she seems to me,—
My bride, my bride that is to be.

I know not if her eyes are light
As summer skies or dark as night,—
I only know that they are dim
　With mystery: In vain I peer
　　To make their hidden meaning clear,
　　While o'er their surface, like a tear
That ripples to the silken brim,
A look of longing seems to swim
　All worn and wearylike to me;
And then, as suddenly, my sight
Is blinded with a smile so bright,
　Through folded lids I still may see
　My bride, my bride that is to be.

Her face is like a night of June
Upon whose brow the crescent-moon
Hangs pendant in a diadem
Of stars, with envy lighting them.—
　And, like a wild cascade, her hair
Floods neck and shoulder, arm and wrist,
Till only through a gleaming mist
　I seem to see a siren there,
With lips of love and melody

And open arms and heaving breast
Wherein I fling myself to rest,
The while my heart cries hopelessly
For my fair bride that is to be . . .

Nay, foolish heart and blinded eyes!
My bride hath need of no disguise.—
    But, rather, let her come to me
In such a form as bent above
    My pillow when in infancy
I knew not anything but love.—
O let her come from out the lands
    Of Womanhood—not fairy isles,—
And let her come with Woman's hands
    And Woman's eyes of tears and smiles,—
With Woman's hopefulness and grace
Of patience lighting up her face:
And let her diadem be wrought
Of kindly deed and prayerful thought,
That ever over all distress
May beam the light of cheerfulness.—
And let her feet be brave to fare
The labyrinths of doubt and care,
That, following, my own may find
The path to Heaven God designed.—
O let her come like this to me—
My bride—my bride that is to be.

94

HOW IT HAPPENED

I GOT to thinkin' of her—both her parents dead and
    gone—
And all her sisters married off, and none but her and John
A-livin' all alone there in that lonesome sort o' way,
And him a blame old bachelor, confirmder ev'ry day!
I'd knowed 'em all from childern, and their daddy from
    the time
He settled in the neighberhood, and hadn't airy a dime
Er dollar, when he married, fer to start housekeepin'
    on!—
So I got to thinkin' of her—both her parents dead and
    gone!

I got to thinkin' of her; and a-wundern what she done
That all her sisters kep' a-gittin' married, one by one,
And her without no chances—and the best girl of the
    pack—
An old maid, with her hands, you might say, tied behind
    her back!
And Mother, too, afore she died, she ust to jes' take on,
When none of 'em was left, you know, but Evaline and
    John,

And jes' declare to goodness 'at the young men must be
      bline
To not see what a wife they'd git if they got Evaline!

I got to thinkin' of her; in my great affliction she
Was sich a comfort to us, and so kind and neighberly,—
She'd come, and leave her housework, fer to he'p out
      little Jane,
And talk of *her own* mother 'at she'd never see again—
Maybe sometimes cry together—though, fer the most part
      she
Would have the child so riconciled and happy-like 'at we
Felt lonesomer 'n ever when she'd put her bonnet on
And say she'd railly haf to be a-gittin' back to John!

I got to thinkin' of her, as I say,—and more and more
I'd think of her dependence, and the burdens 'at she
      bore,—
Her parents both a-bein' dead, and all her sisters gone
And married off, and her a-livin' there alone with John—
You might say jes' a-toilin' and a-slavin' out her life
Fer a man 'at hadn't pride enough to git hisse'f a wife—
'Less some one married *Evaline* and packed her off some
      day!—
So I got to thinkin' of her—and it happened thataway.

WHEN MY DREAMS COME TRUE

I

WHEN my dreams come true—when my dreams
    come true—
Shall I lean from out my casement, in the starlight and
    the dew,
To listen—smile and listen to the tinkle of the strings
Of the sweet guitar my lover's fingers fondle, as he sings?
And as the nude moon slowly, slowly shoulders into view,
Shall I vanish from his vision—when my dreams come
    true?

When my dreams come true—shall the simple gown I
    wear
Be changed to softest satin, and my maiden-braided hair
Be raveled into flossy mists of rarest, fairest gold,
To be minted into kisses, more than any heart can hold?—
Or "the summer of my tresses" shall my lover liken to
"The fervor of his passion"—when my dreams come true?

II

When my dreams come true—I shall bide among the
    sheaves
Of happy harvest meadows; and the grasses and the
    leaves
Shall lift and lean between me and the splendor of the
    sun,
Till the moon swoons into twilight, and the gleaners'
    work is done—
Save that yet an arm shall bind me, even as the reapers do
The meanest sheaf of harvest—when my dreams come
    true.

When my dreams come true! when my dreams come true!
True love in all simplicity is fresh and pure as dew;—
The blossom in the blackest mold is kindlier to the eye
Than any lily born of pride that looms against the sky:
And so it is I know my heart will gladly welcome you,
My lowliest of lovers, when my dreams come true.

NOTHIN' TO SAY

NOTHIN' to say, my daughter! Nothin' at all to
    say!
Gyrls that's in love, I've noticed, ginerly has their way!
Yer mother did, afore you, when her folks objected
    to me—
Yit here I am, and here you air; and yer mother—where
    is she?

You look lots like yer mother: Purty much same in
    size;
And about the same complected; and favor about the
    eyes:
Like her, too, about *livin'* here,—because *she* couldn't
    stay:
It'll 'most seem like you was dead—like her!—But I
    hain't got nothin' to say!

She left you her little Bible—writ yer name acrost the
      page—
And left her ear bobs fer you, ef ever you come of age.
I've allus kep' 'em and gyuarded 'em, but ef yer goin'
      away—
Nothin' to say, my daughter! Nothin' at all to say!

You don't rikollect her, I reckon? No; you wasn't a
      year old then!
And now yer—how old *air* you? W'y, child, not
      "twenty!" When?
And yer nex' birthday's in Aprile? and you want to
      git married that day?
. . . I wisht yer mother was livin'!—But—I hain't got
      nothin' to say!

Twenty year! and as good a gyrl as parent ever found!
There's a straw ketched onto yer dress there—I'll bresh
      it off—turn round.
(Her mother was jes' twenty when us two run away!)
Nothin' to say, my daughter! Nothin' at all to say!

IKE WALTON'S PRAYER

I CRAVE, dear Lord,
  No boundless hoard
    Of gold and gear,
      Nor jewels fine,
      Nor lands, nor kine,
Nor treasure-heaps of anything.—
    Let but a little hut be mine

Where at the hearthstone I may hear
        The cricket sing,
    And have the shine
Of one glad woman's eyes to make,
For my poor sake,
        Our simple home a place divine;—
Just the wee cot—the cricket's chirr—
Love, and the smiling face of her.

I pray not for
Great riches, nor
    For vast estates, and castle-halls,—
    Give me to hear the bare footfalls
        Of children o'er
        An oaken floor,
    New-rinsed with sunshine, or bespread
With but the tiny coverlet
And pillow for the baby's head;
And pray Thou, may
The door stand open and the day
    Send ever in a gentle breeze,
    With fragrance from the locust-trees,
        And drowsy moan of doves, and blur
    Of robin-chirps, and drone of bees,

With afterhushes of the stir
Of intermingling sounds, and then
    The good-wife and the smile of her
Filling the silences again—
        The cricket's call,
            And the wee cot,
        Dear Lord of all,
            Deny me not!

I pray not that
Men tremble at
    My power of place
        And lordly sway,—
I only pray for simple grace
To look my neighbor in the face
    Full honestly from day to day—
Yield me his horny palm to hold,
        And I'll not pray
            For gold;—
The tanned face, garlanded with mirth,
It hath the kingliest smile on earth—
The swart brow, diamonded with sweat,
Hath never need of coronet.

And so I reach,
  Dear Lord, to Thee,
And do beseech
  Thou givest me
The wee cot, and the cricket's chirr,
Love, and the glad sweet face of her.

ILLILEO

ILLILEO, the moonlight seemed lost across the vales—
   The stars but strewed the azure as an armor's scat-
     tered scales;
The airs of night were quiet as the breath of silken sails;
And all your words were sweeter than the notes of
     nightingales.

Illileo Legardi, in the garden there alone,
With your figure carved of fervor, as the Psyche carved
     of stone,
There came to me no murmur of the fountain's under-
     tone
So mystically, musically mellow as your own.

You whispered low, Illileo—so low the leaves were
     mute,
And the echoes faltered breathless in your voice's vain
     pursuit;

And there died the distant dalliance of the serenader's
 lute:
And I held you in my bosom as the husk may hold the
 fruit.

Illileo, I listened. I believed you. In my bliss,
What were all the worlds above me since I found you
 thus in this?—
Let them reeling reach to win me—even Heaven I would
 miss,
Grasping earthward!—I would cling here, though I
 clung by just a kiss!

And blossoms should grow odorless—and lilies all
 aghast—
And I said the stars should slacken in their paces through
 the vast,
Ere yet my loyalty should fail enduring to the last.—
So vowed I. It is written. It is changeless as the past.

Illileo Legardi, in the shade your palace throws
Like a cowl about the singer at your gilded porticos,
A moan goes with the music that may vex the high repose
Of a heart that fades and crumbles as the crimson of
 a rose.

THE WIFE-BLESSÉD

I

IN youth he wrought, with eyes ablur,
   Lorn-faced and long of hair—
In youth—in youth he painted her
   A sister of the air—
Could clasp her not, but felt the stir
   Of pinions everywhere.

II

She lured his gaze, in braver days,
  And tranced him sirenwise;
And he did paint her, through a haze
  Of sullen paradise,
With scars of kisses on her face
  And embers in her eyes.

III

And now—nor dream nor wild conceit—
  Though faltering, as before—
Through tears he paints her, as is meet,
  Tracing the dear face o'er
With lilied patience meek and sweet
  As Mother Mary wore.

MY MARY

MY Mary, O my Mary!
   The simmer-skies are blue;
The dawnin' brings the dazzle,
   An' the gloamin' brings the dew,—
The mirk o' nicht the glory
   O' the moon, an' kindles, too,
The stars that shift aboon the lift.—
   But nae thing brings me you!

Where is it, O my Mary,
   Ye are biding a' the while?
I ha' wended by your window—
   I ha' waited by the stile,
An' up an' down the river
   I ha' won for mony a mile,
Yet never found, adrift or drown'd,
   Your lang-belated smile.

Is it forgot, my Mary,
   How glad we used to be?—

The simmer-time when bonny bloomed
  The auld trysting-tree,—
How there I carved the name for you,
  An' you the name for me:
An' the gloamin' kenned it only
  When we kissed sae tenderly.

Speek ance to me, my Mary!—
  But whisper in my ear
As light as ony sleeper's breath,
  An' a' my soul will hear;
My heart shall stap its beating
  An' the soughing atmosphere
Be hushed the while I leaning smile
  An' listen to you, dear!

My Mary, O my Mary!
  The blossoms bring the bees;
The sunshine brings the blossoms,
  An' the leaves on a' the trees;
The simmer brings the sunshine
  An' the fragrance o' the breeze,—
But O wi'out you, Mary,
  I care nae thing for these!

We were sae happy, Mary!
　O think how ance we said—
Wad ane o' us gae fickle,
　Or ane o' us lie dead,—
To feel anither's kisses
　We wad feign the auld instead,
An' ken the ither's footsteps
　In the green grass owerhead.

My Mary, O my Mary!
　Are ye daughter o' the air,
That ye vanish aye before me
　As I follow everywhere?—
Or is it ye are only
　But a mortal, wan wi' care?—
Syne I search through a' the kirkyird
　An' I dinna find ye there!

HOME AT NIGHT

WHEN chirping crickets fainter cry,
　　And pale stars blossom in the sky,
And twilight's gloom has dimmed the bloom
And blurred the butterfly:

When locust-blossoms fleck the walk,
And up the tiger-lily stalk
The glow-worm crawls and clings and falls
And glimmers down the garden-walls:

When buzzing things, with double wings
Of crisp and raspish flutterings,
Go whizzing by so very nigh
One thinks of fangs and stings:—

O then, within, is stilled the din
Of crib she rocks the baby in,
And heart and gate and latch's weight
Are lifted—and the lips of Kate.

WHEN LIDE MARRIED *HIM*

WHEN Lide married *him*—w'y, she had to jes dee-fy
The whole poppilation!—But she never bat' an
eye!
Her parents begged, and *threatened*—she must give him
up—that *he*
Wuz jes "a common drunkard!"—And he *wuz*, appear-
antly.—

Swore they'd chase him off the place
Ef he ever showed his face—
Long after she'd *eloped* with him and *married* him fer
　shore!—
When Lide married *him,* it wuz *"Katy, bar the door!"*

When Lide married *him*—Well! she had to go and be
A *hired girl* in town somewheres—while he tromped
　round to see
What *he* could git that *he* could do,—you might say, jes
　sawed wood
From door to door!—that's what he done—'cause that
　wuz best he could!
　　　And the strangest thing, i jing!
　　　Wuz, he didn't *drink* a thing,—
But jes got down to bizness, like he someway *wanted* to,
When Lide married him, like they warned her *not* to do!

When Lide married *him*—er, ruther, *had* ben married
A little up'ards of a year—some feller come and carried
That *hired girl* away with him—a ruther *stylish* feller
In a bran-new green spring-wagon, with the wheels
　striped red and yeller:

And he whispered, as they driv
  Tords the country, *"Now we'll live!"*—
And *somepin' else* she *laughed* to hear, though both her
  eyes wuz dim,
'Bout *"trustin' Love and Heav'n above,* sence Lide mar-
  ried *him!"*

HER HAIR

THE beauty of her hair bewilders me—
    Pouring adown the brow, its cloven tide
    Swirling about the ears on either side
And storming around the neck tumultuously:
Or like the lights of old antiquity
    Through mullioned windows, in cathedrals wide,
    Spilled moltenly o'er figures deified
In chastest marble, nude of drapery.
And so I love it.—Either unconfined;
    Or plaited in close braidings manifold;
Or smoothly drawn; or indolently twined
    In careless knots whose coilings come unrolled
At any lightest kiss; or by the wind
    Whipped out in flossy ravelings of gold.

LAST NIGHT—AND THIS

L AST night—how deep the darkness was!
And well I knew its depths, because
I waded it from shore to shore,
Thinking to reach the light no more.

She would not even touch my hand.—
The winds rose and the cedars fanned
The moon out, and the stars fled back
In heaven and hid—and all was black!

But ah! To-night a summons came,
Signed with a teardrop for a name,—
For as I wondering kissed it, lo,
A line beneath it told me so.

And *now* the moon hangs over me
A disk of dazzling brilliancy,
And every star-tip stabs my sight
With splintered glitterings of light!

A DISCOURAGING MODEL

JUST the airiest, fairiest slip of a thing,
  With a Gainsborough hat, like a butterfly's wing,
Tilted up at one side with the jauntiest air,
And a knot of red roses sown in under there
  Where the shadows are lost in her hair.

Then a cameo face, carven in on a ground
Of that shadowy hair where the roses are wound;
And the gleam of a smile O as fair and as faint
And as sweet as the masters of old used to paint
    Round the lips of their favorite saint!

And that lace at her throat—and the fluttering hands
Snowing there, with a grace that no art understands
The flakes of their touches—first fluttering at
The bow—then the roses—the hair—and then that
    Little tilt of the Gainsborough hat.

What artist on earth, with a model like this,
Holding not on his palette the tint of a kiss,
Nor a pigment to hint of the hue of her hair,
Nor the gold of her smile—O what artist could dare
    To expect a result half so fair?

SUSPENSE

A WOMAN'S figure, on a ground of night
    Inlaid with sallow stars that dimly stare
  Down in the lonesome eyes, uplifted there
As in vague hope some alien lance of light
Might pierce their woe. The tears that blind her sight—
    The salt and bitter blood of her despair—
    Her hands toss back through torrents of her hair
And grip toward God with anguish infinite.
    And O the carven mouth, with all its great
Intensity of longing frozen fast
    In such a smile as well may designate
The slowly murdered heart, that, to the last
    Conceals each newer wound, and back at Fate
Throbs Love's eternal lie—"Lo, I can wait!"

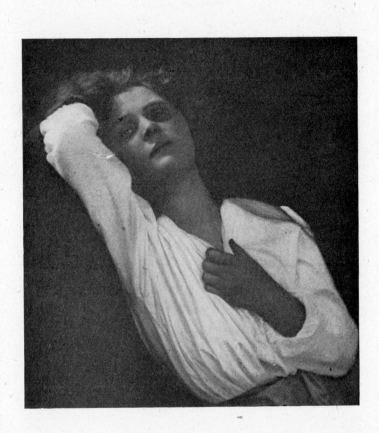

TOM VAN ARDEN

TOM VAN ARDEN, my old friend,
   Our warm fellowship is one
Far too old to comprehend
   Where its bond was first begun:
      Mirage-like before my gaze
      Gleams a land of other days,
      Where two truant boys, astray,
      Dream their lazy lives away.

139

There's a vision, in the guise
  Of Midsummer, where the Past
Like a weary beggar lies
  In the shadow Time has cast;
    And as blends the bloom of trees
    With the drowsy hum of bees,
    Fragrant thoughts and murmurs blend,
    Tom Van Arden, my old friend.

Tom Van Arden, my old friend,
  All the pleasures we have known
Thrill me now as I extend
  This old hand and grasp your own—
    Feeling, in the rude caress,
    All affection's tenderness;
    Feeling, though the touch be rough,
    Our old souls are soft enough.

So we'll make a mellow hour;
  Fill your pipe, and taste the wine—
Warp your face, if it be sour,
  I can spare a smile from mine;
    If it sharpen up your wit,
    Let me feel the edge of it—

I have eager ears to lend,
  Tom Van Arden, my old friend.

Tom Van Arden, my old friend,
  Are we "lucky dogs," indeed?
Are we all that we pretend
  In the jolly life we lead?—
    Bachelors, we must confess
    Boast of "single blessedness"
    To the world, but not alone—
    Man's best sorrow is his own.

And the saddest truth is this,—
  Life to us has never proved
What we tasted in the kiss
  Of the women we have loved:
    Vainly we congratulate
    Our escape from such a fate
    As their lying lips could send,
    Tom Van Arden, my old friend!

Tom Van Arden, my old friend,
  Hearts, like fruit upon the stem,
Ripen sweetest, I contend,
  As the frost falls over them:

Your regard for me to-day
Makes November taste of May,
And through every vein of rhyme
Pours the blood of summertime.

When our souls are cramped with youth
  Happiness seems far away
In the future, while, in truth,
  We looked back on it to-day
    Through our tears, nor dare to boast,—
    "Better to have loved and lost!"
    Broken hearts are hard to mend,
    Tom Van Arden, my old friend.

Tom Van Arden, my old friend,
  I grow prosy, and you tire;
Fill the glasses while I bend
  To prod up the failing fire. . . .
    You are restless:—I presume
    There's a dampness in the room.—
    Much of warmth our nature begs,
    With rheumatics in our legs! . . .

Humph! the legs we used to fling
　　Limber-jointed in the dance,
When we heard the fiddle ring
　　Up the curtain of Romance,
　　　　And in crowded public halls
　　　　Played with hearts like jugglers'-balls.—
　　　　Feats of mountebanks, depend!—
　　　　Tom Van Arden, my old friend.

Tom Van Arden, my old friend,
　　Pardon, then, this theme of mine:
While the fire-light leaps to lend
　　Higher color to the wine,—
　　　　I propose a health to those
　　　　Who have *homes,* and home's repose,
　　　　Wife and child-love without end!
　　　　. . . Tom Van Arden, my old friend.

TO HEAR HER SING

TO hear her sing—to hear her sing—
    It is to hear the birds of Spring
In dewy groves on blooming sprays
Pour out their blithest roundelays.

It is to hear the robin trill
At morning, or the whippoorwill
At dusk, when stars are blossoming
To hear her sing—to hear her sing!

To hear her sing—it is to hear
The laugh of childhood ringing clear
In woody path or grassy lane
Our feet may never fare again.

Faint, far away as Memory dwells,
It is to hear the village bells
At twilight, as the truant hears
Them, hastening home, with smiles and tears.

Such joy it is to hear her sing,
We fall in love with everything—
The simple things of every day
Grow lovelier than words can say.

The idle brooks that purl across
The gleaming pebbles and the moss,
We love no less than classic streams—
The Rhines and Arnos of our dreams.

To hear her sing—with folded eyes,
It is, beneath Venetian skies,
To hear the gondoliers' refrain,
Or troubadours of sunny Spain.—

To hear the bulbul's voice that shook
The throat that trilled for Lalla Rookh:
What wonder we in homage bring
Our hearts to her—to hear her sing!

THE RIVAL

I SO loved once, when Death came by I hid
    Away my face,
And all my sweetheart's tresses she undid
    To make my hiding-place.

The dread shade passed me thus unheeding; and
    I turned me then
To calm my love—kiss down her shielding hand
    And comfort her again.

And lo! she answered not: And she did sit
    All fixedly,
With her fair face and the sweet smile of it,
    In love with Death, not me.

A VARIATION

I AM tired of this!
   Nothing else but loving!
Nothing else but kiss and kiss,
   Coo, and turtle-doving!
      Can't you change the order some?
      Hate me just a little—come!

A VARIATION

Lay aside your "dears,"
 "Darlings," "kings," and "princes!"—
Call me knave, and dry your tears—
 Nothing in me winces,—
  Call me something low and base—
  Something that will suit the case!

Wish I had your eyes
 And their drooping lashes!
I would dry their teary lies
 Up with lightning-flashes—
  Make your sobbing lips unsheathe
  All the glitter of your teeth!

Can't you lift one word—
 With some pang of laughter—
Louder than the drowsy bird
 Crooning 'neath the rafter?
  Just one bitter word, to shriek
  Madly at me as I speak!

How I hate the fair
 Beauty of your forehead!

A VARIATION

How I hate your fragrant hair!
  How I hate the torrid
    Touches of your splendid lips,
    And the kiss that drips and drips!

Ah, you pale at last!
  And your face is lifted
Like a white sail to the blast,
  And your hands are shifted
    Into fists: and, towering thus,
    You are simply glorious!

Now before me looms
  Something more than human;
Something more than beauty blooms
  In the wrath of Woman—
    Something to bow down before
    Reverently and adore.

WHERE SHALL WE LAND?

"Where shall we land you, sweet?"—Swinburne.

A LL listlessly we float
　　Out seaward in the boat
　　　　That beareth Love.
Our sails of purest snow
Bend to the blue below
　　And to the blue above.
　　　　Where shall we land?

We drift upon a tide
Shoreless on every side,
  Save where the eye
Of Fancy sweeps far lands
Shelved slopingly with sands
  Of gold and porphyry.
   Where shall we land?

The fairy isles we see,
Loom up so mistily—
  So vaguely fair,
We do not care to break
Fresh bubbles in our wake
  To bend our course for there.
   Where shall we land?

The warm winds of the deep
Have lulled our sails to sleep,
  And so we glide
Careless of wave or wind,
Or change of any kind,
  Or turn of any tide.
   Where shall we land?

We droop our dreamy eyes
Where our reflection lies
  Steeped in the sea,

And, in an endless fit
Of languor, smile on it
    And its sweet mimicry.
        Where shall we land?

"Where shall we land?" God's grace!
I know not any place
    So fair as this—
Swung here between the blue
Of sea and sky, with you
    To ask me, with a kiss,
        "Where shall we land?"

THE TOUCHES OF HER HANDS

THE touches of her hands are like the fall
    Of velvet snowflakes; like the touch of down
The peach just brushes 'gainst the garden wall;
The flossy fondlings of the thistle-wisp
    Caught in the crinkle of a leaf of brown
The blighting frost hath turned from green to crisp.

Soft as the falling of the dusk at night,
The touches of her hands, and the delight—
   The touches of her hands!
The touches of her hands are like the dew
That falls so softly down no one e'er knew
The touch thereof save lovers like to one
Astray in lights where ranged Endymion.

O rarely soft, the touches of her hands,
As drowsy zephyrs in enchanted lands;
   Or pulse of dying fay; or fairy sighs;
Or—in between the midnight and the dawn,
When long unrest and tears and fears are gone—
   Sleep, smoothing down the lids of weary eyes.

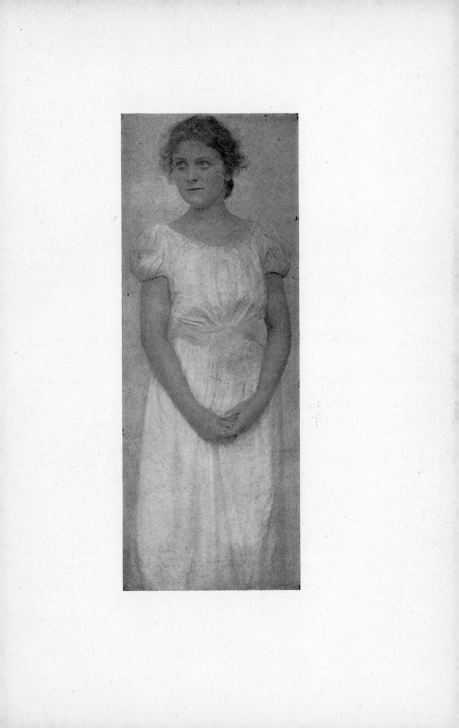

A SONG OF LONG AGO

A SONG of Long Ago:
    Sing it lightly—sing it low—
Sing it softly—like the lisping of the lips we
    used to know
When our baby-laughter spilled
From the glad hearts ever filled
With music blithe as robin ever trilled!

Let the fragrant summer-breeze,
And the leaves of locust-trees,
And the apple-buds and blossoms, and the
    wings of honey-bees,
All palpitate with glee,
Till the happy harmony
Brings back each childish joy to you and me.

Let the eyes of fancy turn
Where the tumbled pippins burn
Like embers in the orchard's lap of tangled
    grass and fern,—

There let the old path wind
In and out and on behind
The cider-press that chuckles as we grind.

Blend in the song the moan
Of the dove that grieves alone,
And the wild whir of the locust, and the
        bumble's drowsy drone;
And the low of cows that call
Through the pasture-bars when all
The landscape fades away at evenfall.

Then, far away and clear,
Through the dusky atmosphere,
Let the wailing of the kildee be the only
        sound we hear:
O sad and sweet and low
As the memory may know
Is the glad-pathetic song of Long Ago!

WHEN AGE COMES ON

WHEN Age comes on!—
    The deepening dusk is where the dawn
  Once glittered splendid, and the dew
In honey-drips, from red rose-lips
  Was kissed away by me and you. —
And now across the frosty lawn
Black foot-prints trail, and Age comes on—
      And Age comes on!
  And biting wild-winds whistle through
Our tattered hopes—and Age comes on!

When Age comes on!—
O tide of raptures, long withdrawn,
  Flow back in summer-floods, and fling
Here at our feet our childhood sweet,
  And all the songs we used to sing! . . .
Old loves, old friends—all dead and gone—
Our old faith lost—and Age comes on—
      And Age comes on!
  Poor hearts! have we not anything
But longings left when Age comes on!

FARMER WHIPPLE—BACHELOR

IT'S a mystery to see me—a man o' fifty-four,
 Who's lived a cross old bachelor fer thirty year' and
  more—
A-lookin' glad and smilin'! And they's none o' you
  can say
That you can guess the reason why I feel so good
  to-day!

I must tell you all about it! But I'll have to deviate
A little in beginnin', so's to set the matter straight
As to how it comes to happen that I never took a wife—
Kind o' "crawfish" from the Present to the Springtime
    of my life!

I was brought up in the country: Of a family of five—
Three brothers and a sister—I'm the only one alive,—
Fer they all died little babies; and 'twas one o' Mother's
    ways,
You know, to want a daughter; so she took a girl to
    raise.

The sweetest little thing she was, with rosy cheeks, and
    fat—
We was little chunks o' shavers then about as high as
    that!
But someway we sort o' *suited*-like! and Mother she'd
    declare
She never laid her eyes on a more lovin' pair

Than *we* was! So we growed up side by side fer thir-
    teen year',
And every hour of it she growed to me more dear!—
W'y, even Father's dyin', as he did, I do believe
Warn't more affectin' to me than it was to see her grieve!

I was then a lad o' twenty; and I felt a flash o' pride
In thinkin' all depended on *me* now to pervide
Fer Mother and fer Mary; and I went about the place
With sleeves rolled up—and workin', with a mighty
    smilin' face.—

Fer *sompin' else* was workin'! but not a word I said
Of a certain sort o' notion that was runnin' through my
    head,—
"Someday I'd mayby marry, and *a brother's* love was one
Thing—*a lover's* was another!" was the way the notion
    run!

I remember onc't in harvest, when the "cradle-in'" was
    done—
When the harvest of my summers mounted up to twenty-
    one
I was ridin' home with Mary at the closin' o' the day—
A-chawin' straws and thinkin', in a lover's lazy way!

And Mary's cheeks was burnin' like the sunset down
    the lane:
I noticed she was thinkin', too, and ast her to explain.
Well—when she turned and *kissed* me, *with her arms
    around me—law!*
I'd a bigger load o' heaven than I had a load o' straw!

I don't p'tend to learnin', but I'll tell you what's a fact,
They's a mighty truthful sayin' somers in a' almanack—
Er *somers*—'bout "puore happiness"—perhaps some
    folks 'll laugh
At the idy—"only lastin' jest two seconds and a half."—

But it's jest as true as preachin'!—fer that was *a sister's*
    kiss,
And a sister's lovin' confidence a-tellin' to me this:—
"She was happy, *bein' promised to the son o' farmer*
    Brown."—
And my feelin's struck a pardnership with sunset and
    went down!

I don't know *how* I acted—I don't know *what* I said,
Fer my heart seemed jest a-turnin' to an ice-cold lump
    o' lead;
And the hosses kindo' glimmered before me in the road.
And the lines fell from my fingers—and that was all I
    knowed—

Fer—well, I don't know *how* long—They's a dim re-
    memberence
Of a sound o' snortin' hosses, and a stake-and-ridered
    fence
A-whizzin' past, and wheat-sheaves a-dancin' in the air,

And Mary screamin' "Murder!" and a-runnin' up to where

I was layin' by the roadside, and the wagon upside down
A-leanin' on the gate-post, with the wheels a whirlin' round!
And I tried to raise and meet her, but I couldn't, with a vague
Sorto' notion comin' to me that I had a broken leg.

Well, the women nussed me through it; but many a time I'd sigh
As I'd keep a-gittin' better instid o' goin' to die,
And wonder what was left *me* worth livin' fer below,
When the girl I loved was married to another, don't you know!

And my thoughts was as rebellious as the folks was good and kind
When Brown and Mary married—Railly must a-been my *mind*
Was kindo' out o' kilter!—fer I hated Brown, you see,
Worse'n *pizen*—and the feller whittled crutches out fer *me*—

And done a thousand little ac's o' kindness and respect—
And me a-wishin' all the time that I could break his
    neck!
My relief was like a mourner's when the funeral is done
When they moved to Illinois in the Fall o' Forty-one.

Then I went to work in airnest—I had nothin' much in
    view
But to drown'd out rickollections—and it kep' me busy,
    too!
But I slowly thrived and prospered, tel Mother used to
    say
She expected yit to see me a wealthy man some day.

Then I'd think how little *money* was, compared to hap-
    piness—
And who'd be left to use it when I died I couldn't guess!
But I've still kep' speculatin' and a-gainin' year by year,
Tel I'm payin' half the taxes in the county, mighty near!

Well!—A year ago er better, a letter comes to hand
Astin' how I'd like to dicker fer some Illinois land—
"The feller that had owned it," it went ahead to state,
"Had jest deceased, insolvent, leavin' chance to specu-
    late,"—

174

And then it closed by sayin' that I'd "better come and
    see."—
I'd never been West, anyhow—a most too wild fer *me*
I'd allus had a notion; but a lawyer here in town
Said I'd find myself mistakened when I come to look
    around.

So I bids good-bye to Mother, and I jumps aboard the
    train,
A-thinkin' what I'd bring her when I come back home
    again—
And ef she'd had an idy what the present was to be,
I think it's more'n likely she'd a-went along with me!

Cars is awful tejus ridin', fer all they go so fast!
But finally they called out my stoppin'-place at last;
And that night, at the tavern, I dreamp' *I* was a train
O' cars, and *skeered* at sompin', runnin' down a country
    lane!

Well, in the mornin' airly—after huntin' up the man—
The lawyer who was wantin' to swap the piece o' land—
We started fer the country; and I ast the history
Of the farm—its former owner—and so-forth, etcetery!

And—well—it was inter*est*in'—I su-prised him, I sup-
pose,
By the loud and frequent manner in which I blowed my
nose!—
But his su-prise was greater, and it made him wonder
more,
When I kissed and hugged the widder when she met us
at the door!—

It was Mary: They's a feelin' a-hidin' down in here—
Of course I can't explain it, ner ever make it clear.—
It was with us in that meetin', I don't want you to
fergit!
And it makes me kind o' nervous when I think about it
yit!

I *bought* that farm, and *deeded* it, afore I left the town,
With "title clear to mansions in the skies," to Mary
Brown!
And fu'thermore, I took her and *the childern*—fer, you
see,
They'd never seed their Grandma—and I fetched 'em
home with me.

So *now* you've got an idy why a man o' fifty-four,
Who's lived a cross old bachelor fer thirty year' and
    more,
Is a-lookin' glad and smilin'!—And I've jest come into
    town
To git a pair o' license fer to *marry* Mary Brown.

THE ROSE

IT tossed its head at the wooing breeze;
　　And the sun, like a bashful swain,
Beamed on it through the waving trees
　　With a passion all in vain,—
For my rose laughed in a crimson glee,
And hid in the leaves in wait for me.

The honey-bee came there to sing
  His love through the languid hours,
And vaunt of his hives, as a proud old king
  Might boast of his palace-towers:
But my rose bowed in a mockery,
And hid in the leaves in wait for me.

The humming-bird, like a courtier gay,
  Dipped down with a dalliant song,
And twanged his wings through the roundelay
  Of love the whole day long:
Yet my rose turned from his minstrelsy
And hid in the leaves in wait for me.

The firefly came in the twilight dim
  My red, red rose to woo—
Till quenched was the flame of love in him
  And the light of his lantern too,
As my rose wept with dewdrops three
And hid in the leaves in wait for me.

And I said: I will cull my own sweet rose—
  Some day I will claim as mine

The priceless worth of the flower that knows
   No change, but a bloom divine—
The bloom of a fadeless constancy
That hides in the leaves in wait for me!

But time passed by in a strange disguise,
   And I marked it not, but lay
In a lazy dream, with drowsy eyes,
   Till the summer slipped away,
And a chill wind sang in a minor key:
"Where is the rose that waits for thee?"

*   *   *   *   *   *   *   *   *

I dream to-day, o'er a purple stain
   Of bloom on a withered stalk,
Pelted down by the autumn rain
   In the dust of the garden-walk,
That an Angel-rose in the world to be
Will hide in the leaves in wait for me.

HAS SHE FORGOTTEN?

I

HAS she forgotten? On this very May
     We were to meet here, with the birds and bees,
As on that Sabbath, underneath the trees
We strayed among the tombs, and stripped away
The vines from these old granites, cold and gray—
And yet indeed not grim enough were they
To stay our kisses, smiles and ecstasies,
Or closer voice-lost vows and rhapsodies.
Has she forgotten—that the May has won
Its promise?—that the bird-songs from the tree
Are sprayed above the grasses as the sun
Might jar the dazzling dew down showeringly?
Has she forgotten life—love—everyone—
Has she forgotten me—forgotten me?

II

Low, low down in the violets I press
My lips and whisper to her. Does she hear,
And yet hold silence, though I call her dear,
Just as of old, save for the tearfulness

Of the clenched eyes, and the soul's vast distress?
Has she forgotten thus the old caress
That made our breath a quickened atmosphere
That failed nigh unto swooning with the sheer
Delight? Mine arms clutch now this earthen heap
Sodden with tears that flow on ceaselessly
As autumn rains the long, long, long nights weep
In memory of days that used to be,—
Has she forgotten these? And in her sleep,
Has she forgotten me—forgotten me?

III

To-night, against my pillow, with shut eyes,
I mean to weld our faces—through the dense
Incalculable darkness make pretense
That she has risen from her reveries
To mate her dreams with mine in marriages
Of mellow palms, smooth faces, and tense ease
Of every longing nerve of indolence,—
Lift from the grave her quiet lips, and stun
My senses with her kisses—drawl the glee
Of her glad mouth, full blithe and tenderly,
Across mine own, forgetful if is done
The old love's awful dawn-time when said we,
"To-day is ours!" . . . Ah, Heaven! can it be
She has forgotten me—forgotten me!

BLOOMS OF MAY

B^{UT} yesterday! . . . .
    O blooms of May,
And summer roses—Where-away?
O stars above,
And lips of love
And all the honeyed sweets thereof!

185

O lad and lass
And orchard-pass,
And briered lane, and daisied grass!
O gleam and gloom,
And woodland bloom,
And breezy breaths of all perfume!—

No more for me
Or mine shall be
Thy raptures—save in memory,—
No more—no more—
Till through the Door
Of Glory gleam the days of yore.

THE SERMON OF THE ROSE

WILFUL we are in our infirmity
  Of childish questioning and discontent.
Whate'er befalls us is divinely meant—
Thou Truth the clearer for thy mystery!
Make us to meet what is or is to be
With fervid welcome, knowing it is sent
To serve us in some way full excellent,
Though we discern it all belatedly.
The rose buds, and the rose blooms and the rose
Bows in the dews, and in its fulness, lo,
Is in the lover's hand,—then on the breast
Of her he loves,—and there dies.—And who knows
Which fate of all a rose may undergo
Is fairest, dearest, sweetest, loveliest?

Nay, we are children : we will not mature.
A blessed gift must seem a theft; and tears
Must storm our eyes when but a joy appears
In drear disguise of sorrow; and how poor

189

We seem when we are richest,—most secure
Against all poverty the lifelong years
We yet must waste in childish doubts and fears
That, in despite of reason, still endure!
Alas! the sermon of the rose we will
Not wisely ponder; nor the sobs of grief
Lulled into sighs of rapture; nor the cry
Of fierce defiance that again is still.
Be patient—patient with our frail belief,
And stay it yet a little ere we die.

O opulent life of ours, though dispossessed
Of treasure after treasure! Youth most fair
Went first, but left its priceless coil of hair—
Moaned over sleepless nights, kissed and caressed
Through drip and blur of tears the tenderest.
And next went Love—the ripe rose glowing there
Her very sister! . . . It is here; but where
Is she, of all the world the first and best?
And yet how sweet the sweet earth after rain —
How sweet the sunlight on the garden wall
Across the roses—and how sweetly flows
The limpid yodel of the brook again!
And yet—and yet how sweeter after all,
The smouldering sweetness of a dead red rose!

190